# THIS TIME I AM GOING TO GET IT
# RIGHT

◆

## MAKE SURE YOU DON'T FORGET
## TO USE YOUR RESOURCES

## LOUISE CHILDS

iUniverse, Inc.
Bloomington

**This Time I Am Going To Get It Right**
**Make Sure You Don't Forget To Use Your Resources**

iUniverse books may be ordered through booksellers or by contacting:

iUniverse
1663 Liberty Drive
Bloomington, IN 47403
www.iuniverse.com
1-800-Authors (1-800-288-4677)

ISBN: 978-1-4502-9657-1 (sc)
ISBN: 978-1-4502-9658-8 (ebk)

Printed in the United States of America

iUniverse rev. date: 02/11/2011

*"To all of those who are motivated to*
*get to where they are going because, they know where they have been."*

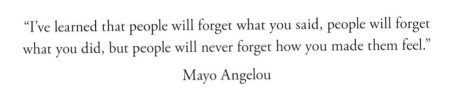

"I've learned that people will forget what you said, people will forget what you did, but people will never forget how you made them feel."

Mayo Angelou

# Contents

# The Bridge Builder

An old man, going a lone highway,
Came at the evening, cold and gray,
To chasm, vast and deep and wide,
Through which was flowing a sullen tide.
The old man crossed in the twilight dim;
The sullen stream had no fears for him;
But he turned when safe on the other side
And built a bridge to span the tide.

"Old man," said a fellow pilgrim near,
"You are wasting strength with building here;
Your journey will end with the ending day;
You never again must pass this way;
You have crossed the chasm, deep and wide --
Why build you the bridge at the eventide?"

The builder lifted his old gray head:
"Good friend, in the path I have come," he said,
"There followeth after me today
A youth whose feet must pass this way.
This chasm that has been naught to me
To that fair-haired youth may a pit-fall be,
He, too, must cross in the twilight dim;
Good friend, I am building the bridge for him."

Will Allen Dromgool

# Preface

These thoughts have been a part of my life for many years. This is my opportunity to share my experiences and my thoughts with people who have not gotten as far as I have and neither have a path to go forward. I am humbled to be able to provide an opportunity for anyone who needs to take the first step.

Your path will enlighten you of things that you have never thought possible. I have been able to achieve things that broaden my horizons and my learning experiences by following these edicts. Learning is such a wonderful experience. It will provide you with fulfilled dreams and a life of happiness forever. Enjoy!

# Acknowledgements

I would first like to thank God, for his patience and untiring unfeigned love for which he has given to me unconditionally. He has fortified me to go through the vicissitudes of life and he never left me without a solution. The lifeline God was willing to supply; it was I who refused his guidance to lead me down the right path. It was I who had to recognize that without God, I can do nothing.

Additionally, I would like to thank every company that I had applied for an employment opportunity and was denied. You pushed me to use my life experiences, coupled with my college education and continued course of studies to turn my impossibilities into possibilities. Rejection allowed me to go back to the drawing board to improve my game. "If there is no struggle, then there can be no progress."

Most importantly, I want to thank my family members who believed in me. I now understand that in this life, everyone is not for you and you may have to walk alone. When you become self-actualized you begin to learn that you have potential.

A special thanks to my mother, Rosa R. Garcia. I love you girl. You are my greatest cheerleader. Whenever I felt like throwing in the towel, my mother wouldn't let me. She shared her stories about her struggles with me and how she overcame her obstacles. How's that for determination?

To my twin brother Louis Childs, hey Bro, I love our stimulating conversations and I appreciate your honesty and our closeness.

To my sister Marsha E. Neely, love brought us back. People will try to tell you how they think our story is going to end, but little do they know, they weren't there when the story began. Our story has an ellipse and not a period. Together we stand and divided we will fall. Let's continue to stand united, that's the truest test of all!

To my children, son-in-law and grandson: Qualita Diaz, Sona Abdon, Ines Nieves and Edward Abdon, and my grandchildren: Justin and Leila Abdon. I thank God for all of you. I am blessed to have successful daughters and an intelligent grandson and son-in-law in whom I am well pleased. Stay assertive and focused and remember to keep God first and he will deny you nothing.

To my grandparents the late Mr. Booker T. Neely Sr. & Mrs. Pearl L. Neely, thank you for being the example that I can proud to emulate. You were salt to the earth and a beacon of light for the entire world to see. Shine on!

To my cousin Sandra Neely, you have always been an inspiration to me. I will never forget the encouraging words that you spoke to me, you said Louise, "stop worrying about the grade and take the class." Those words still resonate with me to this very day!

To my uncle, the late George Horace Neely, thank you for seeing me as a diamond in the rough. He knew of my potential and through his social contacts he was able to network to give me an opportunity to experience the exciting life of Runway Modeling at the age of fifteen. He knew then that I had abilities and talent to be shared with the world.

# Introduction:

"Change your perspective and your perspective will change."

I knew that I had a story that I wanted to tell and I wasn't quite sure about the platform in which I would deliver my message so I have chosen to write it instead. What I was profoundly sure of is that, "when the teacher is ready, then the students would come." I'm ready. I have been completely flabbergasted about this journey that I have embarked upon and as the late poet writer, Langston Hughes once said, "Life for me isn't been a crystal stair, but I have been a climbing!" I can certainly relate to this euphemism. My life resembled a labyrinth, a tortuous arrangement that is difficult to find your way. I don't know about you, but that's an uncomfortable feeling and not having a clear and decisive path, you can wind up anywhere. This leads me to why I've chosen to be candid about writing this self-help, instructional how-to mini book. The title of my book: "This Time I Am Going to Get It Right: *Make sure you don't forget to use your resources*, was so appropriate and easy to write because, it tells my story about my life experiences of trying so hard to get "it" right. I think that the biggest crime that you can commit against yourself is not recognizing your true potential. I believe that I was called to achieve excellence and not mediocrity.

You often would hear the experts say, anything that you enjoy doing in life, then that is your purpose. Guess what? I've enjoyed interior designing, I've enjoyed being an avid traveler, and I've enjoyed sewing and cooking. I've enjoyed being an entrepreneur but because I've enjoyed these things, what was I supposed to become was my question that I had asked myself repeatedly only to come up emptied handed. The problem was not with what I wanted to do as much as it was for me trying to figure out how to navigate my way towards obtaining my true purpose, was most challenging. This was my major concern.

How many times have you heard people say, oh baby, don't worry about it, you just keep doing what you are doing and you will get there. Eventually you will, until you're the ripe old age of Methuselah! No one is living that long anymore! It can be quite cumbersome and mind taxing when you are not given the proper guidance or clear cut directions as how to achieve your goals. You're in a complete tail spin; it's like a dog chasing his tail. What do you hope to accomplish by doing that; I am sure that one thing you will get and that is a headache. Well, in order for you to have peace of mind while pursuing your dreams try these immeasurable intangibles: have clarity, a decisive plan and a strategy. With these ingredients, it will make pursuing your purpose a lot easier and enjoyable. You can grow, when you know.

Making your dreams come true require work and effort, and if you don't mind the hard work that goes into making your dream come to fruition, you'll gladly look back and say, I've not labored in vain, I can see the fruit of my labor. As for me, I would rather keep trying and fail, then to do nothing and be declared a failure for not trying at all.

Triumph and be an overcomer. If you sit and do nothing, then expect nothing. You're goals are obtainable, but that's not the issue, what matters is having the proper tools in place in order for you to effectively reach them.

# Chapter 1

* ◆ *

# Louise's Story

"There is a way that seems right, but at the end it could be totally wrong and destructive." I've heard this bible verse being quoted repeatedly during my childhood and until I became an accountable and responsible adult. There is something to be said about doing something the right way versus doing it the wrong way. What feeling do you get from doing something right versus doing something inaccurately? There is a feeling of joyfulness that you experience when you've scored well on a test or when you've accomplished a goal and when you've finished a race. What are the feelings that you experience, when you've bombed a test or failed to complete or achieve a goal? There is a feeling of despair and disappointment when you've fallen short of successfully attaining your objective. How much preparation time went into planning and developing your goals and objectives? Was there a realistic quantitative timeline that help you to measure your progress toward obtaining your goals and objectives? These questions are extremely important to consider implementing when designing a plan. If you keep these questions on the forefront, they will help you to stay on task with your plans.

Without direction or a plan, you tend to find yourself wandering aimlessly. You've heard the question asked "what is the perfect law of insanity?" The answer is doing the same thing over and over again while expecting different results. Now you see why no progress is being made? We first have to figure out what it is that you want to do and how do you expect to get from one objective to the next. If you are not assessing these key elements, then do not expect the outcome to be favorable. Knowing and understanding what your goals and objectives are may require work, but if you're tired of coming up emptied handed then you have to make the necessary changes toward reaching your intended aim. I have made a lot of promises to myself and each time I promised myself that I would get it right. I was excited, but each time my excitement was short-lived because, I didn't have clarity, a plan or a strategy and all of these items play an integral role toward obtaining your goals, which is the end result. I had product, but I didn't implement a plan that would allow me to execute my strategy. I know by now you're probably saying to yourself, my goodness, you were a fool! I would like to resort to being a bit impulsive, but the truth of the matter is up for interpretation. Of course anyone should know that before you to start anything you have to a roadmap and a compass, if you don't you are doomed for gloom. However, you aren't thinking about that at the time, all you want to do is to get started and then at the halfway point, you find yourself running out of fuel. You're no longer motivated because you do not understand how to get the golden egg. Nothing seems to be working, you're tired, you're frustrated and disappointment sets in and you become discouraged. I've been there too many times and the sad part about the story is that I didn't quit, I just jumped right back into doing something different, but with the same behavior. Some of you are shaking your head in disgust, but I am literally laughing while writing this story because, I have come to an understanding and that there are two kinds of people God looks after and they are fools and babies. They don't know any better. Thank God he was looking after me, I can hear him clearly say to me Louise,

I have the utmost confidence in you, you will figure it out eventually and eventually I did just that.

There is good news for those who have experienced goal upsets or drawbacks. It is clearly evident to me now, that if you expect to move forward with your goals, you have to do the basics. Pull yourself back from venturing down the wrong path. You can achieve your goals successfully; your goals can be easily obtainable, but first things first. We often become unglued and detached from reality of having what we want and the reason I perceive this to be from my very own experience is this – a lack of knowledge. In addition to that, I wasn't taught how to be a successful entrepreneur. What was instilled and drilled into me was this, "you can be anything you want to be in this life." Oh yeah? That may be a statement of fact, but is it a statement of truth? Being told that I could do or become anything in life was motivating, but it didn't help me to connect the dots. In my mind I was still disjointed. How do you suppose that I can do and become whatever I want in this life, if I am not shown or given the tools to do so? Are you serious? That's why I've decided to share my story. I am not saying that it can't be done, what I am suggesting is this, if you don't have a plan and a strategy of execution, for your dreams to come to fruition, they will be delayed or inhibited. Then here comes disappointment tapping on your shoulder only to remind you, that you forgot to implement the important ingredients that were necessary to carry out your dream. You can be your worst enemy by not heeding the necessary steps to achieving your goals or your own best friend by deciding to follow the important steps of making better informed decisions. Disappointments will come, but there is no need of giving it a front row seat when disappointment can be avoided by making the right decisions toward goal achievement.

There is a purpose for which you were designed to fulfill, and if you aren't cognizant of how to bring your purpose to surface, then it will lie dormant inside you until you're able to acquire the tools to make your God-given talent become a reality. If you don't know how to turn your dream into a reality then that can be a true struggle for anyone to take on. As for me, my struggles have been my challenges and my challenges have been my struggles, together they have forced me to reexamine my direction and choose a better course of action. It is very easy to relinquish your dreams when your vision is obscured, that's the easy way out. Turn your weaknesses into strengths and your threats into opportunities; the way to accomplish this task is that, you must be willing to acknowledge that you've missed the mark. Most assuredly numbers do not lie, if you are keeping count. If you have to make some adjustments to your plan, the time and effort that it takes to perfect your plan is well worth it. Do not stress over the fact that you had to make changes to your plan and that by doing so your projection date toward your goal will be delayed. I would rather delay the date for reaching the intended objective in order to get it right, than to ignore the changes and have your plan announced that it was dead on arrival. There is work involved in getting what you want and it requires action! I guess you're going to have to look at Mr. Lazy and say "you're fired!" "Nothing comes to a sleeper, but a dream." It's all right to dream, but now it's time to put some feet on those dreams and get them moving and it requires a plan. Are you fired up yet? I hope so. Every plan that you have developed and designed requires your attention, there is nothing wrong with a having a written plan, you need it. You can go back as many times as necessary to revisit your plan and make the needed changes that is required to perfect your plan and strategy. However, I would like to caution you, that without a viable plan to work with, your ideas will be just like a balloon, they'll be up in the air. You have to keep the plan in plain view and once changes have been made then you can let go of the string. Your plan, can now take the direction it needs to go. There is a right way in which you can pursue your goals. Develop and design a plan and follow it.

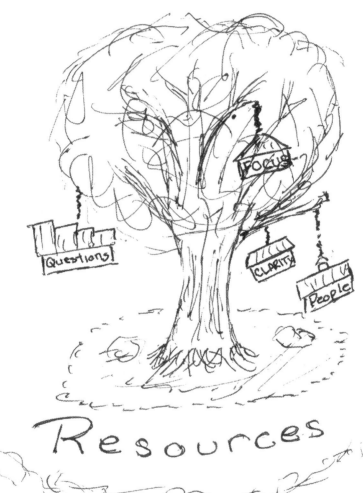

Resources

# Chapter 2

* ◆ *

# Use Your Resources

I feel like Tim the tool man and even this television character realized that if you're going to make something you need the proper tools to do it. I've served in the United States Army for twelve years as Intelligence Analyst. There were times I had to go on road marches and there were times it required me to have a map and a compass for me to reach a certain bench mark within the allotted time of a training exercise during the road march. There was no way possible for me to reach the intended objective without the instructional aides that were provided for me to successfully complete my mission. Without the tools, reaching my objectives would have been inhibited. By the way, another soldier accompanied me during the mission. It's called the buddy system, even in the military no man is an island, you have to be interdependent. You have to be able to communicate and collaborate which brings me to another topic regarding the title of this book. Using your resources is vital to any mission. Without having your resources the mission becomes once again, impeded or inhibited. The modus operandi becomes compromised; the task cannot be completed because you do not have the resources to get started, let alone finish. How do you expect to get it right, if you don't have the proper tools in place? We have been made aware that the tools that are needed for the objective to be realized are a written plan, a well developed blueprint, clarity and a strategy. Additionally, there are more physical resources which need to be used. Whatever your desires or interests are, they can be achieved. I believe in sharing information as to how to make your dreams come true. Here's how we can make our dreams possible. Through research and I know that may seem boring to you, but just how serious are you in pursuing your goals? It requires that you do something. Visit your local library, research material regarding your topic of interest. Then you can extend your search through a virtual library called the Internet. That's right! There is so much information housed by the Internet, you can find just about anything you want. When using your computer when accessing the Internet, you're just a click away from obtaining the information that is needed to get you one step closer to your objective.

If you are looking for a shortcut, then you can forget it. I've learned earlier on in life that there are no shortcuts and if you wind up taking a shortcut, you'll end up paying for it in the long run. When you spend the quality time to make what you want happen, the work may seem long and tedious, but I assure the reward will be even sweeter. You have to sacrifice some things in order to get what you want in life. Do you mean I have to put that boyfriend on hold in order to make my dreams come true? If he is more than liability, than an asset, then yes. After you've accomplished your goal alone, you may not want him to partake of the fruit of your labor. If he or she wasn't there before, during or after, then no thank you, but that's another chapter in a different book. The point that I am trying to make is you have to remain true to your calling. Stay focused. I was just kidding about the boyfriend; you can keep the deadbeat around. Jokingly, get rid of your distractions! Now that I've gotten that off my chest, did you know that people are your greatest resource of information? If you want to know how something is done, why not ask the person who has already has a successful track record. They can share tips with you as to how they got started, which will include a prospectus. Create a laundry list of questions, an inquiring mind always wants to know, become inquisitive. So many important tips can be shared from the expert peer, if only you were to ask them. The more questions you ask, the closer you get to your goal-attainment.

Let me ask you some questions? What do you want to accomplish in your life, what are your short-term and long-term goals toward your objective, and how do you expect to reach them? Do you have clarity? Do you a decisive plan? You can no longer afford to be aimless about the goals you wish to pursue in life. Even if you're going to school, please ensure that you have a career path and do not pursue an education just for the sake of having one. How will the education be used, once it is obtained? Do not misunderstand me, education is the greatest equalizer there is, and without it you're lost. Anything you want to know, from the simplest to the most complex issue requires that you educate yourself regarding that topic of interest. What I am saying is this, you need to know or at least have an idea of what it is you want to do, and how to go about designing and developing a plan, before you start your venture.

Assess the situation. Stop putting the cart before the horse. Assessment plays an integral role of determining whether the steps that is being made toward the objective is adequate. Assessment helps you to keep your finger on the pulse when making an informed decision of what changes if any are necessary to be made to improve the quality of instruction regarding goal attainment. It took me a while to figure out this whole entire process, but once you have been enlightened with the information, one can only become empowered to make the changes that are needed to get the wheels turning. I believe that "the more you know, the more is required of you to grow."

# Chapter 3

• ◆ •

# Strategy

Moving forward, the next phase to be concerned with is devising a workable strategy. How do you intend to carry out your plan? Do you think that you will need a strategy? How else will you get from one place to the next? Nothing just automatically happens, the thought has to be well planned out and once you've planned it, how do you expect to carry it out? Is there one strategy or will there be many needed strategies? That all depends on the individual and what they are trying to accomplish. However, just like a teacher in a learning environment, there is no one-size-fit-all solution, there is no magic bullet. You probably need to exercise multiple strategies in order to see what strategy is the best. Mediocrity is not an option. We are going after what works the best. You may have to dig deep to find the best answers to support the best strategy toward goal achievement. Get the shovel and let us begin to go below the surface. Sometimes the answers are always on the top of the surface. You may have to break the surface in order to get what you want. Hard work is not for the timid. If you don't want to break a sweat, then this chapter is not for you. However, since all of the steps are vital in reaching your goals and objectives there is no way that this section should be ignored. Accomplishing any goal in life requires work and if there is no deposit, then you can best believe that, there will be no return. You have to be willing to invest in yourself, your dreams and in your future! Construct an airtight comprehensible strategy that will place you on the right path of pursuing your interests. This is where I am, but this is where I need to go or by this timeline I plan to reach my objective within this timeframe and then you devise a strategy that will get you there. If only I knew what I know now. However, it is a comforting feeling that when you know better you do better. No matter how old you are, you still have a chance of making your dreams come true. What are you waiting for, certainly not an invitation?

Do you have your shovel handy because you are going to have to start digging for answers? You will have to brainstorm to find solutions. You will have to be willing to burn the midnight oil or you will need to burn the candle at both ends. You will need the tripartite pillars of a network of friends and family members who can impart wisdom, provide constructive advice and the haters, who I refer to as the bottom feeders; they are there to keep you motivated because they already believe that you can't achieve what you've started. So, you need them too. I want you to be able to visualize your dreams. Can't you just see it? Don't you believe in it? Do you remember when you were a child and you played the game of hopscotch. In order to beat your opponent you had to toss a coin, or stone into a diagram which consisted of ten squares. Your strategy was to toss the device into the square with just enough speed and subtlety in order to land in the right block, in order for you not to forfeit your turn to play. You were careful while you were hopping not to step on the any of the lines within the blocks or land in block that had a coin or a stone inside of you. You had to repeat the same method when you had to turn around and pick of your stone, head back down to square one. That took skill and strategy. You have jumped from one square to the next and you got there and picked up the coin or the stone and returned. That is the way a strategy works. It gets you moving in the direction you need to go. A strategy is result driven and that is what you should experience with a strategy – results.

How bad to do you want to taste success? How bad do you want to breathe, well that's how bad you have to want success. If you're breathing, then you can succeed. What does breathing have to do with anything? You're alive aren't you? That means you can get started with what you want to do with your dreams and aspirations. When the dirt is thrown over your body, that's when it's too late for you to fulfill anything. It's over, but even when it is all said and done, what legacy did you leave behind? I hope it will tell a story that you lived and made a conscionable contribution to your family and society. What type of statement will your life make?

It's so important to know where you are going and most importantly how to get there. Being clueless is undoubtedly by far, the worst feeling that anyone could encounter. I know for a fact being clueless makes me feel uneasy, unsure and uncertain. So I try as best and hard as I can to stay abreast of the status of my progress. What's your strategy, how do you plan to get to the next level or go to the next phase of instruction without a strategy, you won't. You have to be in it, to win it. Go for it!

# Chapter 4

• ◆ •

# Focus

"Do not be weary in well doing, because in due season you will reap, if you do not faint." This bible verse speaks volumes. It resonates within my mind to stay focus on what I want to pursue in life. You cannot waver, you may get discouraged, but that is just a feeling and you will get over it. There are a couple of stories that I loved reading when I was little girl and even today as an adult, I will revisit the story to help me to regain my focus. The message then is still prevalent today. Do you remember the story of the "Fox and the Grapes" You may be wondering what does this fable have to do with the title of this book. It has a lot to do with the title, author and her message. The story of the "Fox and the Grapes" speaks to those who want to taste the fruit of their labor without the essential elements of constructing a plan and a well thought out strategy. He sat there and stared at the grapes and if he had used his resources, he would have then been able to obtain them. If he wanted them bad enough he could have gotten a ladder, he could have asked for help, but because he did absolutely nothing, he had considered the grapes to be sour. How many of us have displayed that type of attitude toward wanting something and because it was not within our reach, we developed a negative attitude about the very thing that we strived to obtain? Opportunity doesn't fall into your lap; one who seeks opportunity must prepare with the proper tools to complete his goals. When you're not prepared for the opportunities that life can present to you, you may hear comments from your friends or family members massage your ego by telling you, "child do not become discouraged and beat yourself up about not getting, that job or that bank loan to open up your business, when it is meant for you to get it, it will happen, just you wait and see. Or better yet, God knows exactly what it is that he wants you to do, and in due time, he will tell you exactly what it is. Huh? I have never heard anything so remotely ridiculous in all my life. Keep waiting dear, and you will discover that God's word clearly said that he has given you the power to achieve your goals. When you achieve a wealth of knowledge, it will help you to achieve your goals. Do you have a blueprint? How do you plan to get from point A to point B without a plausible strategy? I do believe that the ball is in your court and it takes faith along with a defined strategy to get the ball rolling and if you do not have one, the ball will remain unplayable. If telling you the truth no matter how raw it can be, it will help you to get motivated and moving in the right direction. I do not believe in being roundabout, which may be one of the reasons why progress is not being made towards reaching your goals. Tell me anything about myself; just don't tell me the truth. Truth is a powerful tool, it can hurt you and turn around and heal you. Embrace the truth, once it is said, you feel better. However, there is a requirement, make positively sure that when we give constructive advice, do it in the spirit of meekness and in love! Without following the requirement, there is no guarantee that your advice will be received.

Do you want to be like the sly clever fox that was not able to reach his grapes and determined that the grapes were sour? Sometimes life allows us to rewrite our story, especially when a valuable lesson has been learned. I have been the fox, but I never said that the grapes were sour. I remained focused and I kept trying until I was able to discover what it was that I wanted to obtain. I have to admit, the grapes of opportunity are pretty juicy.

GOALS
5 miles
CRITICS
GUTS
moving
company
Failure
5 miles
The WAY
To your goals!

# Chapter 5

• ◆ •

# Get Moving!

Are you still on the fence about your decision to get moving with implementing your goals and objectives? Get behind the wheel and get moving. Progress cannot be made by looking through the rear view mirror. You have to look through the front window if you want to get moving. I am sure that you can think of a myriad of reasons that may keep you from reaching your goals, and I am sure that fear and its' cronies may be holding you captive. You have to loosen their grip and demand them to flee. Move in the present and forget those things which are behind and reach toward the prize. The prize is the end goal and you are not going to receive the prize if you do not take the steps to get started. This can be a daunting task, but nothing good comes easy and if it did, wouldn't everyone be doing it? It takes guts to get the ball rolling, but it can be done. You have what it takes to get moving, do not second guess yourself, you have been given practical, common sense solutions that can help you make better informed decisions about how to get moving toward pursuing your goals.

Sometimes I think that we praise our obstacles, more than we praise our efforts in trying to surpass them. Thinking on the obstacles keeps us on the fence and our dreams become stifled. You can no longer afford to procrastinate, doodling your dreams away is no longer allowed. You have to take ownership of what you want to do and how you expect to get there, but if you do not take the steps to move in the right direction, then your ideas will remain just dreams. Eventually you will have to get out of your comfort zone and get moving and remember you are never alone. I am providing you with the moral support and tools and resources that will help you to get moving with pursuing your goals. I know what it feels like to be on your own and not having the know-how. The results can be dramatically devastating and that is why I am here for you! Your success matters to me and that is why I am in your corner cheering you on and I am literally telling you, Come On, I know you can do it, It's mind over matter, but most importantly you now have the keys to get you where you need to be: clarity, a plan and a strategy.

What else do you need? A shove and my boot! Get moving! Excuses are for the lame and for the weak and they have not right to reside in you. Push them aside and get your hide in for the best ride of your life.

I have more advice that I wish to share with you in order to get you moving. I want to encourage you not to concern yourself about the pace. The pace should be a slow and steady. Do you remember the fable about The Hare and the Tortoise? It is true, I want you to get moving, but do not be overwhelm yourself about the speed, slow is good. When moving toward pursuing your goals, take your time. Now that you are moving in the right direction, you don't want to become rushed. You can become sloppy and careless and miss some important lessons when you're on the go. You have a suggested timeline and if you should happen to fall short of reaching that mark, do not despair, stay on course and you will get there. Always be willing to improve your game. I have learned that if you have to compete, be willing to compete against yourself first.

Do not listen to the critics, they were not there when you were befuddled, they didn't lend a hand to help you to figure it out even when you knew they had the information that could have made a difference. I think that they were satisfied in seeing you chasing your tail. You know what it is like in being in the eye of the storm; the good thing is, the wind does not always blow in the same direction. There is calm after the storm. You have become smarter, wiser, empowered and enlightened about the information that you lacked before. What a relief? It is refreshing to have a sense of direction and I share those feelings with you. I guess when life throws you a lemon, and then you can make lemonade and not only make it, but drink it too! Nothing seems to bother you when you have made the right decisions concerning your goals. Your attitude changes and you feel that you can take on any challenge. Your obstacles and challenges become so minute. You began to tell yourself, there is nothing that I can't accomplish, I am an overcomer and that you really are too.

# Chapter 6

• ◆ •

# Life is a Journey

I like to consider myself as a late bloomer, but I have blossomed wherever I was planted, I just didn't enjoy the soil. The soils were my choices. When I reflect back over my life I am amazed of how much I have grown. I thank God for this. You cannot begin to understand of the many inner struggles that I faced head on. The feeling of being inadequate discombobulated, not connecting the dots, being impatient, and jumping from one thing into another, no stickability. "Oh wretched man that I am who shall deliver me from my anxieties?" This was my life and my life was not always this complicated. Trying to find my purpose was. I was unhappy within. Until one day, I began to make sense out of all of the rubbish that I had taken myself through. Admitting your faults is cathartic. Not blaming anyone else for my shortcomings is being the adult. I have heard within my own family of suggestions of not being successful was due to circumstances or certain selfish individuals holding them back from achieving their goals, are you kidding me? At the end of the day, someone has to be the adult and say, I am my own biggest problem and that I cannot run from myself. Man up! They were still successful, but I am not sure if they lived out their true potential. This chapter grants me an opportunity to face my demons and tell myself that you have been set free from the chains that once had you bound. I ask myself, why I allowed myself to take the paths that I did. Why did I journey down this road? How did I get on this boulevard? "When you don't know what path to take, any path seems right." I do not mind being transparent, hopefully my message will resonate with those who are also trying to figure out this thing, called life. I am here to tell you, you can!

I had to stop worrying about the grade and I had to take the class was the advice that my cousin Sandra had given me many years ago. I never forgot what she told me, I just forgot to apply it. We are our worst critic, but I am my own best friend, which the two seems to balance out each other quite well. I would often ask myself, what is the lesson that I am supposed to learn? Believe me; you will not go to the next level until you do. No one else's formula can work for you. Your path has been inexplicably designed for you to take and no one can take the journey for you. We all have to be accountable for our own actions in life and out of the accountability a story is told.

I wrestled with my angel just like Jacob did, and I vowed that I was going to figure it out. This time I am going to get it right! You have to be still in order for your inner man to speak. What is meant by that? Reflect! Go back to the beginning of where the confusion started and fix it, by acknowledging it and taking the proper measures to avoid repeating the same errors. How can you go wrong with having clarity about what it is you want out of life? Are having a plan and a strategy and resources inconceivable? Can you build a house without a plan? Of course you can, but just think how great the collapse will become of that house without building it without a blueprint? Even you will become perplexed in trying to figure out, what the heck it is.

Do your homework, be willing to put your nose to the grind stone and roll up your sleeves and be prepared to get dirty, get to the nitty gritty and forget the "as easy as one, two and three crap." If you want something done right you have to have the proper tools in place that will help you accomplish what you've started. If you want successes then you have to take the initiative and have the drive and the discipline to start and complete the process from the very beginning to the very end. In addition, while I am on the roll, don't buy into the hype of believing that there is no one-size-fit-all strategy. It is a lie! When you plant a seed, isn't there a process? When you build a company, isn't there a process? When a mother is pregnant and is expecting her baby to arrive, isn't there a process? All right then, come on somebody, then why do you expect to reach your dreams, goals and objectives in a week? It takes time. You have to perfect the gift that is in you. With perfection you have to be willing to go back and make necessary changes until you get it right.

Start with the basic essentials: clarity, a plan, a strategy and your resources. These are the tools in which to build your foundation. All other ground is sinking sand, "the winds and storms came and blew upon the house and great was the fall of it." There goes your dream! Avoid the dream collapse, use the proper ingredients and you'll see results. Take one step at a time and during this journey, you will begin to appreciate the strides that you are making towards your goals. You have to assess your progress and keep your fingers on the pulse to monitor the outcome. Do you need to make any adjustments to your plan? Is the timeline that you wish to accomplish your goals foreseeable and obtainable? Are you doing it right this time? Are you pleased with the results? I hope so.

I was insatiably determined that I had a lot of fight left in me and that while on this journey, I was going to turn something's around and get a grip on life and ride it, because like a ghost I was tired of it riding me. You cannot expect different results if you hadn't changed your behavior of doing the same thing over and over again. If the plan is broke, then expect broken results. What you put in, is what you will get out. "Whatever a man sows that shall he also reap." It is important that you take your time to do the thing right if you expect to get a return on your investment.

Do you think that there is no light at the end of the tunnel? There will be times that you will want to relent, but you've come too far to not to go the distance. The only time when you should throw your hands up is when you are crossing the finish line in victory! Remain committed to your goals and dreams. "Persistence is the omnipotent!" Having a defeatist attitude is not allowed on this journey. Tell the defeatist attitude to take a back seat for a change; you're in the driver's seat, where you belong and there is no way for you to reach your destination if you don't take charge of eradicating your man-made obstacles. Stop shifting, stop postponing your dreams, you have the ability to win.

I realized that while being on this journey, there is not a single approach to reaching your dreams, you come to grips and be at peace with yourself when you discover that there are multi-faceted approaches that you will have to take in order to see your dream materialize. That's the beauty of this journey, you learn the valuable lessons that life offers you. I embrace the lessons that I've learn wholeheartedly. As I have become older, I feel a sense of peace about the choices that I've made and that I was able to go back to the drawing board until I was able to figure it out. As a student of life and a college graduate and a continuous lifelong learner, I have learned that there are all sorts of learners; some learners are quick and some slow. When the lesson finally clicks in, you get it. You have a lot of fast learners, who have done absolutely nothing with their talent, except to bury it and you were in competition with them? For what reason might I ask you? "I have learned whatever state that I am in, be content."

You've tried everything that you could and you still have come up empty however, the operative word is tried. You may have taken some blows, you've received a lot of no's. There are times when you wanted to yell, scream and ask yourself "why me?" Why not you? You have been conditioned, you have been fortified and even though you feel as though you have been thrown under a bus, you got back up and brushed yourself off and said I'm not through. I've done it wrong, now it's time to learn how to get it right, what do I do? How do I get there? What is the education that I need? What are the skills that I need to acquire? Being on the journey allows you to question your behavior and take definitive measures to correct the wrong. You mean to tell me that I have been going the wrong way for these last twenty-five years? Some critics will challenge me and make comments such as: "I think you should go easy on yourself" or "You sure are your worst critic" and how about this one "Give yourself a break, we've all made mistakes and no one is perfect." I say, don't placate the truth, be honest with yourself, don't excuse the truth for a lie. If the dress is ugly, then say it. Don't make excuses as why you haven't gotten it right, you know why you haven't gotten it right. The only person that you cannot lie to is yourself. You know the issues and the reasons that underline your shortsightedness. I quote Shakespeare, "To thine own self be true" in other words Boo-Boo, you know you.

Now that you realize what the purpose of the journey is for, isn't it just tragic for those who have no clue. I remember sitting in church in Philadelphia, Pa, one Sunday morning and I heard the Pastor say "If a man knows not and he knows that he knows not, this man can be helped and if a man knows not and doesn't know that he knows not, this man is a fool. Finally, if a man knows and knows that he knows, this man is wise, follow him! I now know, that I know, that I know. What a relief that is – "to know!"

I took me sometime "to know" what I now know and it's made all the difference in the world. The cataracts have fallen off and I can see so clearly now. I have always walked to the beat of my own drum, I don't consider myself to be a traditionalist or a slave to convention and I love that about me, but somehow along the way, I just couldn't figure out, what my true calling was. Of course, I've been a lot of places and I've done a lot of things, but there was such a longing tugging inside me to want more. Along this journey, I wanted to dig, analyze develop and foster what the "more" is for me. It's been a gratifying experience and the experience has been this, there is no one solution, there are multiple ones, so if something doesn't work, then it's okay to try something else. I've learned to be content with things that I have, being full and with being empty. I have learned that no one has a monopoly on knowledge; no one can know it all. No one was born smart; they were conditioned to be that way. Intervention can be applied at all levels, you are never too old to learn and you can teach an old dog new tricks, you just have to be accommodating to their needs.

While on this journey there is another important factor that I want you to consider, and that is, if you "change your perspective, then your perspective will change." You have the power within you to win and what you need to do is to tap in.

# The Road Not Taken

Two roads diverged in a yellow wood
And sorry I could not travel both
And be one traveler, long I stood
And looked down one as far as I could
To where it bent in the undergrowth;

Then took the other, as just as fair,
And having perhaps the better claim,
Because it was grassy and wanted wear;
Though as for that the passing there
Had worn them really about the same,

And both that morning equally lay
In leaves no step had trodden black.
Oh, I kept the first for another day!
Yet knowing how way leads on to way,
I doubted if I should ever come back.

I shall be telling this with a sigh
Somewhere ages and ages hence:
Two roads diverged in a wood, and I-
I took the one less traveled by,
And that has made all the difference.

Robert Frost

# Chapter 7

. ◆ .

# Where is your faith?

What is tiny, but when it is exercised the results can be extremely enormous? Did you guess the right answer? If you said faith, then you are absolutely correct! The size of faith is as tiny as a mustard seed. You mean my faith doesn't have to be the size of the Taj- Mahal or the Grand Canyon? No! The faith size requirement is the size of a mustard seed and that is very, very small. The seed may be small, but you can think big and that is all you need to do. For those who want to convince you that is takes a big leap of faith to get what you want in this life, it doesn't. There are others who will try to make you feel guilty about how much faith you need, just because they may be sitting high and looking low. Take comfort and know that, you can have faith as the size of a mustard seed to move a mountain. Did you ever stop to think that, that is the reason why you are still standing? You have the faith to stand even when the odds are against you – stand anyway!

Speak to your mountains of fear, doubt, and of lack and tell yourself, that this time, I am going to get it right. This time I am going to win!

The more you hear something, the more you are prone to believe it, how else do you think faith comes, it comes by hearing:

"Watch your thoughts; they become words.

Watch your words; they become actions.

Watch your actions; they become habits.

Watch your habits; they become character.

Watch your character; it becomes your destiny."

# Chapter 8

◆

# The Engine That Would

I am not the engine that could, but I am the engine that would. Would what? Eventually get it right! I had to understand the significance of getting it right and what it meant to me and how it intensified me to take immeasurable responsibility for my actions. You would think that one certain thing that you do should bring success to your life, but ultimately if you're anything like me who enjoy the many splendors that life brings, you want to take an advantage of the opportunities. While on my track to discovery, I wondered if I had taken several tracks which would derail me from my destination. Ultimately it would delay me from reaching my objective, but if no objective was ever defined, then I was enjoying the ride and there is certainly nothing wrong with that. However, the tragedy is repeating the same behavior. Do you want precision or would you rather prefer a collision? If you choose the latter than you just might get it. Depending upon where you want to go in life I would suggest that you make some well thought out plans, create a decisive strategy with clarity, then implement and execute them. "How can we walk together, except we agree?" You have to be in agreement with yourself to succeed or else you will find that your trip to discovery will be cut short. My experiences in life may be similar or different from yours, but whatever they are I am here to remind you that there is "nothing new under the sun," we've all experienced obstacles, pitfalls, poor choices that we had to accept. We had to put the past behind us and eventually move on or be stepped on. No one likes to revisit their skeletons just to put meat back on their bones. My skeletons are telling me to do so. What drove me to write this book is that one day, I would be the engine that would figure out. Instead of aimlessly being on the track, I knew that I would have direction. Instead of worrying if I was on the track while on my journey, I would come to appreciate the scenic route that only the tertiary tracks could provide. You read of my struggles, now you may read of my successes. What is success? For me, it is a liberating experience to know that if I would have taken a lot more time to think about what I wanted when I was a teenager, then I could have spared myself from a lot of disappointments. You began to compensate for your losses and you will do just about anything to find or a way to be successful. I joined the military, didn't really want to do that, but I had to make the best out of an opportunity that I didn't wish to embark upon. I jumped in and out of network marketing, but it wasn't meant for me. I had lot of hobbies, I loved to travel and that was interesting to me because I saw a lot of things and I experience different cultures. I made a lot of things with crafts: jewelry, pillows, painting and sewing but I didn't sell the items and I could have because they were beautiful, unique one of a kind item. I could have capitalized monetarily off of my many talents, but when you don't have a plan then you accumulate a lot of stuff. I have learned from my experiences, I should have had a plan. The next time I choose to sell lemonade, I will choose the right corner first. All of things that I've experienced aren't wasted but they were put on standby until I was able to revisit them and devise a plan to capitalize on the past efforts. For me, this is success.

Everyone has a different definition of what success is and as for me, it's the toil and sweat, it's the disappointments and the tears, but through it all you can look back and say, I made it and that's what counts. No matter how hard the journey has been, I didn't quit. Have I completed my path, no I'm just like you, I'm ever evolving. I am not preaching from the pulpit. I am part of the audience. The difference is I have taken the sunglasses off and I have seen my goals. I have clarity, a decisive plan and a strategy. I am completing my education; I am investing in my future. I have put my plans together; I have formed a strategy and I drive a Ford Focus and I'm focused on creating my own success. For those who continue to toil at finding their correct path, now is the time for you to find out what the heck you were born to do! You know what, I am finally proud of myself.

# Afterword

Somehow we want to explain why we did not accomplish what we started, but I am not here to make excuses. I am here to encourage those, that if you're serious about achieving your goals, it is going to take discipline to see your goals come to fruition. You have to have stickability to see your project to the very end. Get a strong support system, people who you can rely on. If you are not a leader then you can be taught to become one. Once you've discovered the answers then it is time to get moving. Pour yourself into what you want to do. Seek after it, crave it, study it and understand it.

# Epilogue

Do you have a goal? Do you have a dream? Some dreams come true and some do not. What good is it to have a dream if you do not take the proper measures to nurture it? As your friend I have made it my purpose to share my instructional tips that will inform you and transform your thinking so that you can change your direction. I want to hear from you about the strides that you are making toward your goals. It's time for you to use your shovel to break up your fallow ground, turn over a clean slate and start afresh and anew. ☺

My email address is lc.newslate@gmail.com. Let me know how this self improvement book has helped you. Additionally, I have created a blog, http://leweez-newslate.blogspot.com/2010/12/its-not-over.html.

My blog is designed for you to share your tips, ideas or your experiences that helped you to get started on your venture. Sharing your information can be useful to others who need an extra push to get them motivated to move in the right direction. A curious minded person normally gets the answers that they are searching for and an ordinary thinker sometime does not. Be unique and ask the questions that are needed to move you to the next phase of your plateau. As a graduate and an ongoing student, I have learned about how other cultures have a strong support system. When sharing life experiences, the education between the cultures become enhanced. Everybody learns well from that experience. Countries such as Korea, Japan, China, and Mexico practice in collectivism. Collectivism is sharing the experiences so that it enhances the whole. When knowledge is shared it benefits the community and the benefit makes the community better.

On the other hand, in my experiences the older generations prospered from collectivism, the new generations have not adopted collectivism. The current communities do not rely on their neighbors. In the past, the neighbors made the communities and were mentors. Without their mentors they become plumb dumb or they get themselves in a blind corner because they don't know where to turn.

Let's get back to the basics. Every strong building needs a strong foundation. Every individual needs firm footing. Both physically and mentally you must be able to stand strong. To be able to do that, you need a strong community base, and mentors that will point you in the right direction. These are the tools that are necessary for every person to succeed. Without these failure is guaranteed. Everybody has to get on the carousel of life, they have to learn how to reach and grasp the brass ring. What is the brass ring? It is the goals that the individual wishes to achieve. Not everyone wants to be a doctor, not everyone wants to be a lawyer, but somebody wants to be the best at whatever they choose to be. How can I help you? I think that I have already placed you on your best path. Now it is up to you to put your best foot forward and make the best out of everything you have been blessed with. Shake off the cobwebs, come out of your cocoon, your wings are no longer restricted, so open them and fly. You've hung around long enough. That's so not cool! You are a butterfly, you were born to fly. Your dreams will die, if you do not give them a purpose. You've dreamed enough and now it is time to get moving. Emancipate yourself; you are the only one who can.

# Conclusion

"Be anxious for nothing." Take your time and remain consistent when pursuing your goals. "The race is not given to the swift and neither to the strong, but to him who endures to the end." When you know where you are going the end is clear in sight. When you're impulsive, rambunctious and befuddled, your dreams will be delayed. You have to get from under the debris within your mind and or your surroundings and tell your inner man to be still. Choose a quiet place and collect your thoughts and ensure that you have your computer or a pencil and a notepad handy. You have some work to do.

I would tell you not to concern yourself with what is going on with our economy, but what I will suggest is that regardless how tumultuous or how volatile our economy may be, you have reinvent yourself to fit into the economy. Do not throw caution to the wind. Study the market, find out if there is a need for your niche` and not your itch. The itch may make you understand that there is something to scratch about. Ask yourself important hard line open ended questions that require a critical response instead of a yes or no answer. Do not rush yourself into thinking that if you do not rush and hurry yourself with what you want to accomplish, you'll miss your opportunity. Not so. If you hurry and rush, then the likelihood of getting your goals accomplished will have more flaws then you can imagine. I choose accuracy over quantity any day and so should you. Don't worry, "he who procrastinates is lost," not the one who is making remarkable strides to reach their goals at the pace of a turtle. Even Heinz ketchup is "slow good." So, take your time to ensure that you have clarity, a plan and a strategy. The cost of these elements is simply your valuable time. Use it wisely!

# About the Author:

Louise Childs is an Afro-American who was born and raised in Philadelphia Pa. She served proudly in the United States Army as a Non-Commissioned Officer. She held two occupations while serving in the United States Army; she was an Intelligence Analyst and also a Chemical Specialist. She served in the first Gulf War; Desert Shield/Desert Storm.

In March of 2004, at the age of forty-four, Louise Childs pursued a four year college degree in Business Administration with a minor in Management at Strayer University in Morrisville, North Carolina. Louise Childs graduated Magna Cum Laude with a 3.84 GPA. Additionally, Louise Childs embraces education as a lifelong learner; she decided to continue her education at North Carolina Central University in Durham, North Carolina, where she is currently enrolled in the Teacher's Licensure Certification Program.

Louise says that education is the greatest equalizer and with having an education, it opens the door of opportunities, you just have to be on the right side of the door when it opens. This leads me to the reason I wanted to write this book. Being on the right side of the door doesn't mean just knocking on a company's door, what about your own door? Do you hear the inner voice which tells you to get started creating or building your own business? There are so many talents that reside inside of everyone and those talents are untapped. I started to dig and

I found many talents that I could pursue. I have provided you with the essential ingredients: clarity, a plan and a strategy. These key elements are an integral part to your foundation to help stabilize your footing and provide a bridge for you to cross.

When information is shared and someone is giving you a hand up, doesn't it make sense to reach for it and grab it? Give yourself the permission to succeed. I thank God for the many gifts that he has imparted in me to share with the world. Someone is counting on you to help them through and if you' use your talents the person will get the help that they need.

My friend, no longer do you need to be disheartened, through intervention you are in the right place at the right time. A lifeline has been thrown, take hold of it and live. You can make it, I know you can!

What are Louise's future goals? Becoming a Motivational Speaker and starting an Outreach Program to mentor the youth and help literacy program at a literacy program for "At-Risk" groups. This has always been my goal to fulfill. Nothing is impossible for those who believe, and I believe. I believe in my ability to lead people into finding their goals. I believe that my efforts will make a difference. Most importantly, doing continuous research will help to uncover new methods to achieve my goals. If you continue to use the same method or strategy, you will not find new ways to improve the paths to your goals. It is self evident that, I practice what I preach. Just as a reminder, there is a solution for every problem that you may encounter in your life. Use your tools which are your resources, and do not be afraid to admit that you may not always know the answer. When you act as if you know it all and you do not, then it will slow the process considerably. If you do not know, this is the time to use your resources. There is no shame in not knowing, but there is shame in pretending to know.

## "There's Gift that Lies in You"

A song created by: Louise Childs

There's a gift that lies in you yes it does, yes it does, there gift that lies in you yes it does. It was given just for you, from above, from above; it was given just to you, from above. Will you see your gift through and through, through and through, through and through; will you see your gift through and through, it's up to you. Will you allow your gift to die and never care or wonder why? That's a shame because your gift is so important.